NEAR WATER

Text copyright © Claire Llewellyn 2006
Illustrations copyright © Mike Gordon 2006

First published by Hodder Children's Books in 2006

Reprinted in 2006

Editor: Kirsty Hamilton
Designer: Peter Bailey, Proof Books

Llewellyn, Claire
Look out near water
1.Drowning - Prevention - Pictorial works - juvenile literature
I.Title II.Gordon, Mike III. Near water
613.6

Printed in China

ISBN-10: 0340 894407
ISBN-13: 978 0 3408 9440 8

Hodder Children's Books
A division of Hodder Headline Limited
338 Euston Road,
London NW1 3BH

LOOK OUT!
NEAR WATER

Written by Claire Llewellyn
Illustrated by Mike Gordon

Hodder
Children's
Books

a division of Hodder Headline Limited

Do you like
playing in
the bath,

splashing through puddles,

4

Here I come!

or jumping in the paddling pool?

Then you'll know
that water can
be lots of fun.

5

But have you ever fallen
under water, lost your
breath and nearly choked?

Then you'll know that water
can be frightening, too.

Some animals can breathe under water... or hold their breath for a very long time.

Turtle

8

But people can't.
Under water, they stop breathing
and after a minute or two they die.

This makes water very
dangerous indeed.

We all need to be careful with water.
Where is the water in your home?

Is there water in the garden?

Do you sometimes go to the swimming pool?

It's important to learn how to swim – though it can take a little time.

Week by week you get a little bit better, and then suddenly –

But even when you know how to swim, you still need to be careful in the water.

It's important to think about others, too.

What could happen if you jumped on your friends or pushed them into the water?

In summer it's fun to swim in the sea.
Is this like swimming in a pool?

The sea is strong, and it
is always moving.

It can drag things out to sea.
It could carry you away.

Don't go after it!
I'll buy you another.

My ball!

Some beaches are safer than others. They have flags to show where it is safe to swim and lifeguards to watch over people.

But even so, you must take care
and never ever swim alone.

19

In summer, if the sea is far away, you can go to a river or lake.

You can fish...

...or paddle,

or take a boat
out on the water.

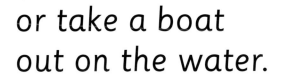

21

But the weather can quickly change.
One moment, everything is fine.

Then, suddenly, the sky clouds over...

and a wind begins to blow.
Now the water is very choppy.

Rivers and lakes are cold and deep.

If something went wrong, and you fell into the water, it would be very hard to swim.

A life-jacket helps to keep you afloat while someone rescues you.

What would happen if you didn't wear one?

Take extra care when you're near a river.

Many rivers are deep
and fast moving.

Do you think they're a
good place to swim?

Everyone enjoys playing with water.

Most of the time water is fun,
but it can be dangerous too.

Never put yourself or a friend in danger.

Notes for parents and teachers

Look Out! Near Water and the National Curriculum

This book will help cover elements of the PSHE curriculum at KS1 (ages 5-7), in particular the requirement that children at this age "should be taught rules for, and ways of, keeping safe ... and about people who can help them to stay safe". The Citizenship KS1 and KS2 schemes of work are also relevant. Activities relating to the scheme of work unit entitled 'People who help us – the local police' could include personal safety elements.

Issues raised in the book

Look Out! Near Water is intended to be an enjoyable book that discusses the importance of safety in and around water. Throughout, children are given the opportunity to think independently about taking care of themselves and about what might happen if they do not pay attention to safety issues. It allows them time to explore these issues and discuss them with their family, class and school. It encourages them to think about safety first and about the responsibility and practical steps they can take to keep themselves safe.

The book looks at the things we do in and near water, including baths, garden ponds, swimming pools, lakes, rivers and the sea. It explains the potential danger of water and asks questions about how children feel about water, and what might happen if someone falls in.

It is also full of situations that children and adults will have encountered. It allows a child to ask and answer questions on a one-to-one basis with you. How does it feel to be splashed by water? How does it feel to fall in water? Have they ever been frightened in this way? Are they learning to swim? How do they feel about going in the sea? The illustrations provide amusing and helpful ideas.

Being safe in or near water is important for everyone. This book tackles many issues. It uses open-ended questions to encourage children to think for themselves about the consequences of their behaviour.

Suggested follow-up activities

Think of animals that live in ponds, rivers and the sea. Which ones can breathe under water? Draw a picture of one or two of these.

What sort of things sink and float? Make a collection of objects and see if they will float in a bowl of water. How do people stay afloat in the swimming pool if they cannot swim?

Draw a picture of a beach on a summer's day. Add a lifeguard and some flags to the beach to show where it is safe to swim.

The Royal Society for the Prevention of Accidents (ROSPA) has a useful and informative website including fact sheets: www.rospa.com

Books to read

Safety First By Water (Franklin Watts, 2004)

Look Out by Water (Evans Brothers, 2003)